CHICAGO BULLS

AARON FRISCH

Published by Creative Education
P.O. Box 227
Mankato, Minnesota 56002
Creative Education is an imprint of The Creative Company.

DESIGN AND PRODUCTION BY **ZENO DESIGN**

PHOTOGRAPHS BY Getty Images (NBAE)

LIBRARY OF CONGRESS CATALOGING-IN-PUBLICATION DATA

Frisch, Aaron.
Chicago Bulls / by Aaron Frisch.
p. cm. — (NBA champions)
Includes index.
ISBN-13: 978-1-58341-505-4
1. Chicago Bulls (Basketball team)—History.
2. Basketball—History. I. Title.

GV885.52.C45F75 2007
796.323'640977311—dc22   2006020237

9 8 7 6 5 4 3

COVER PHOTO: *Point guard Kirk Hinrich*

THE BULLS are a professional basketball team in the National Basketball Association (NBA). They play in Chicago, Illinois. Chicago can be cold and windy. It is nicknamed "The Windy City."

Chicago is a big city with many tall buildings ▷

5

6

THE BULLS' arena is called the United Center. Their uniforms are red, black, and white. The Bulls play lots of games against teams called the Bucks, Cavaliers, Pacers, and Pistons.

◁ The Bulls started playing more than 40 years ago

THE BULLS played their first season in 1966. One of their best players was guard Jerry Sloan. He always hustled and played tough defense. The Bulls were a good team, but they could not win the NBA championship.

Jerry Sloan always played as hard as he could ▷

9

10

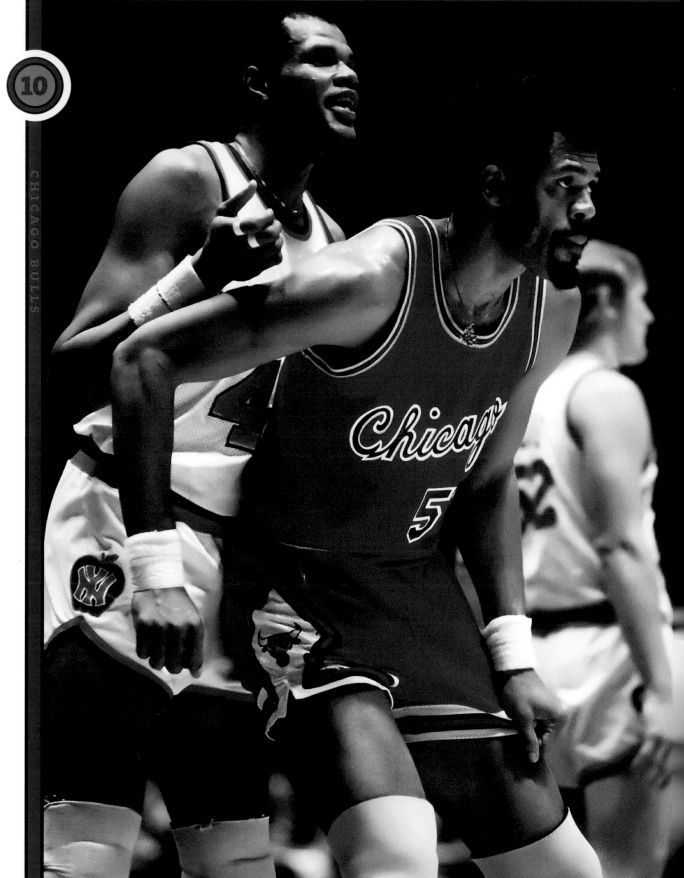

THE BULLS' next star was a center named Artis Gilmore. He was more than seven feet (213 cm) tall and blocked a lot of shots. Fans called him "The A-Train."

◁ Artis Gilmore blocked 1,748 shots in the NBA

11

IN 1984, the Bulls got a new guard named Michael Jordan. He became one of the best basketball players ever. He could jump so high that people called him "Air Jordan."

It was very hard to stop Michael Jordan ▷

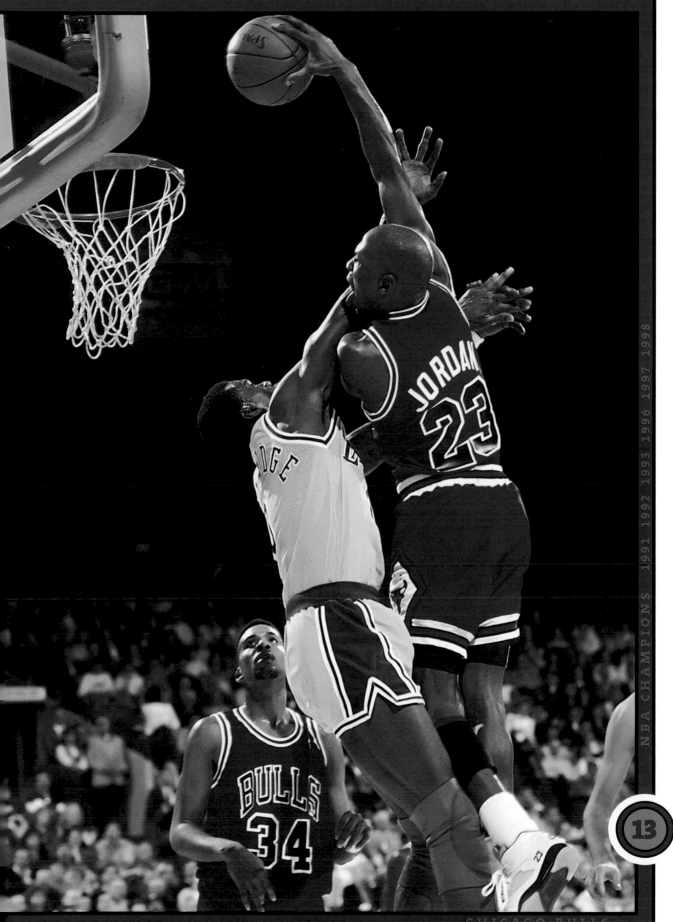

13

14

JORDAN and forward Scottie Pippen made the Bulls one of the top teams in the NBA. But they kept losing in the playoffs to a team called the Pistons.

◁ Scottie Pippen played 12 seasons in Chicago

15

16

IN 1990, Chicago got a wise coach named Phil Jackson. The Bulls finally beat the Pistons and then won the NBA championship. They won the championship the next two years, too!

Coach Phil Jackson had smart plays for the Bulls ▷

17

18

MICHAEL JORDAN retired after that, and the Bulls got worse. But two years later, Jordan came back. He made the Bulls great again. In 1996, they won 72 games and lost only 10! The Bulls won the NBA championship again in 1996, 1997, and 1998. But then Jordan quit for good.

◁ Bulls fans had parties after every championship

KIRK HINRICH *[HINE-rik]* was another good Bulls player. He was a point guard who made smart passes and played tight defense. The Bulls have many new players today. Chicago fans hope that their team will win the NBA championship again soon!

Kirk Hinrich was a good passer and team leader ▷

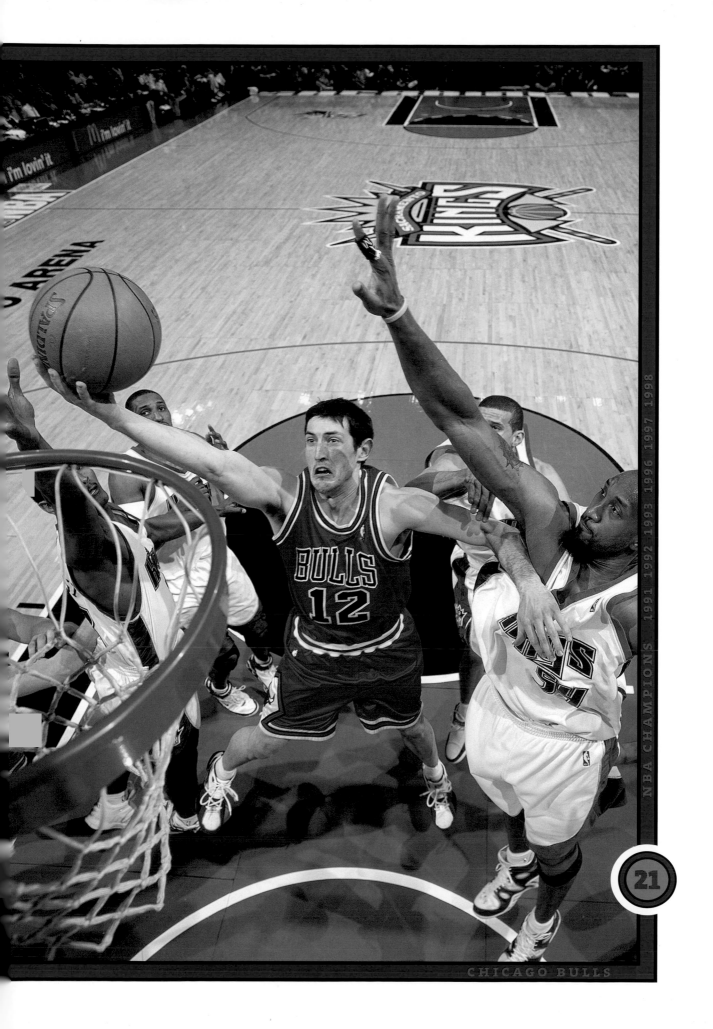

21

GLOSSARY

ARENA   a building with lots of seats where teams play basketball

NATIONAL BASKETBALL ASSOCIATION (NBA)
a group of basketball teams that play against each other; there are 30 teams in the NBA today

PLAYOFFS   games that are played after the season to see which team is the best

PROFESSIONAL   a person or team that gets paid to play or work

RETIRED   stopped playing for good

FUN FACTS

TEAM COLORS: Red, black, and white

HOME ARENA: United Center

CONFERENCE/DIVISION: Eastern Conference, Central Division

FIRST SEASON: 1966

NBA CHAMPIONSHIPS: 1991, 1992, 1993, 1996, 1997, 1998

GREAT PLAYERS: Jerry Sloan (guard), Michael Jordan (guard), Scottie Pippen (forward)

NBA WEB SITE FOR KIDS: http://www.nba.com/kids/

TEAM NAME: The Bulls got their name because people used to sell cows and bulls in Chicago. Bulls are very strong animals.

INDEX